COLD ANGEL OF MERCY

COLD ANGEL OF MERCY

poems by

AMY RANDOLPH

RED HEN PRESS ❦ LOS ANGELES 2002

ACKNOWLEDGEMENTS
Some of the poems in this collection first appeared in the following
magazines and publications: "A Light Will Come On Without Warning" in
Lullwater Review; "Easter Sunday" in *Painted Bride Quarterly*; "Moon" in *En Plein
Air*; "Beach Winter" in *Peregrine*; "Angel" *Black Warrior Review*.

Cover artwork: "La Cellule d'Or" (The Golden Cell) by Odilon Redon.
© Copyright The British Museum

Book and cover design by Mark E. Cull

ISBN 1-888996-55-2
Library of Congress Catalog Card Number: 2002100486

Published by:
Red Hen Press
www.redhen.org

FIRST EDITION

PRINTED IN CANADA

for Ruth Stone

Contents

IV

V

VI

VII

COLD ANGEL OF MERCY

I

Angel

I go back to January, back to the farmhouse
with its soft golden eyes, the dog pens
and fallen fence posts gloved in snow.

This is where a woman gets buried late at night,
over and over, under the blindness
of stars, wind clapping in the ears. There are lanterns,
picks and shovels, the crush of heavy shoes.

They come slowly, carrying her body
which sings from the far edge
of a deep pasture. I love the ones who do this to her.
It is right; and all around her a reaching, the wilderness leaning

toward tires and garden tools,
clothespins dangling like hagsteeth. The moon, approaching descent,
spills its cold milk on the backs
of the laborers. They are afraid of her pallidity
against their darkness, afraid because what grows in them

trembles like the edge of a great wing. I name her "angel"
or "self." Beyond the fenceline, a thin sheet of snow
rises like a bride's veil. This is home, such grief and unfolding.

A Light Will Come On Without Warning

She says let's talk now
about old flames. Let's
                    measure them up. In a single breath,

her gray, smoke-filled
breath, a past life, leans forward,
                    as reflection. There are the eyes

of my former husband, ripe
with bad omens. Somewhere
                    he walks with his head down

and my name tattooed in blue letters
on his chest. This was love
                    at twenty-one, solid

as a brick wall. I feel now
like a ghost singing.
                    Listen. We are sitting here,

two women, but I know
what sometimes happens over coffee, between hours
                    of half-serious talk and dreaming. We might

change our names, our skins. We might decide
suddenly that life here could be better
                    there, in a small town up north.

But she's older, knows how to stay
where it all began. I know
                    I want a beer and my own corner

of a crowded dance hall. But the waiter won't come
anytime soon. He has strong bones in his face
                    and many friends. I have a son

waiting at home, sleeping soundly with the name
I gave him while a late snow pressed the glass
    of the window, gathering quietly

like faces. Outside the sidewalks shine
with rain. I wait for her voice
    to place my body in its own light.

Driving Highway 80

How vigilantly the egrets look north, straight into the sharp
        eyes of rain, white necks bright as candles
in a field of black dirt and dried pieces
of cornstalk.

        I am driving to you from the far side of this wind
that promises colder mornings
in the coming days. Over the next rise, smoke twists upward

like a broken sail. A trailer home burns
under a ring of clouds that are as useless as the one fire engine
heading to meet the flames.
        At the edge of the field,
children turn circles like joyful, barefoot spirits.

Easter Sunday

Families are resurrected
in sunlight. Another family man, drunk,
sleeps in the grass
on his side. I believe in something

now and then, feel a larger body,
older, walk through
a secret door in me. I read

your letter, see in my hands
the island you live on. I open the door,

walk through, knowing I am in love with this distance
that makes us look harder for the body,
the tangible light of skin.

How to Bring Beauty to Such Acts

Dante,
but this isn't the *Paradiso*, the needle
sinking again, me
in my nightgown again, hopeless Beatrice

      saying come out

of the bathroom, the baby kicked and the day
grows vivid. There is blood,
minutest of valentines
in the sink, on the buckling
floor. Where is grace? Not
in these hands, but somewhere

      between the dwindling soul

and the body's great need, in here
with the worn-through bedcover, out there
with the goats in the yellow field,
where there is no sign of rain.

      I want fire,

just a small flame to lick
at the edges, to see this life go final
and exquisite as smoke.

Living Inside the Body

1
In the endless cave of the body,
where stars burn without light,
where one soul presses up against another, hungry:
perhaps one lives too long in the dead-end corridors
of the hands.

2
The body can break open
with a single thought, as water
finds fissures in smooth walls.

Year by year, the body falls in
until it becomes its own black mirror.

3
I see the face of my mother,
surprised, like an animal lifted to sit among saints
in their tattered robes.

Self-Portrait Inspired by a Reproduction
of Van Gogh's "Houses at Auvers"

A woman is frozen
halfway between those two most painful
steps, where tenths of seconds

slow, like mothwings
becoming touchable, and leave her

open to each delicate
death. What has happened
here—first, to turn her head away from her flowers,

the wandering Jew,
and then to stop her, the plastic
watering can tilted in her hand, a single drop of water
poised on the lip of the spout
above three violet blooms—

is the instance of a voice coming from inside
another room. Her name
drifts out to her, and all its hard moments

when need turns slowly
from plant to child to the door
leading out, the window with its frightening face
of other windows. *On the whitewashed wall*
above the peperomia, a figure, hunched,
crooked,

is set forever to take his next step.

Cemetery from a Train Window, Somewhere in Texas or The Day I Left My Husband

They plunge up among headstones, through
drought-hardened dirt,
                wiry buttercups, wine cups,

and black-eyed Susans. Beyond the dead,
black cows graze a yellow field,
                black holes

eating stars. I don't know what happens to a voice,
silk cheek, or strong and stubbled chin,
                when a life walks back into itself

with a lonesome gait,
not a word.
                Farther south, from where I've come,

cactus flowers are just starting to bloom,
big sloppy kisses that tell you as you go, "Goodbye, goodbye.
                I love you. Goodbye."

II

Harvest Moon, Cornfields, Dirt Road

White-skirted moon, barefoot moon,
       cuts across the field, unlocking
the eyes of that doe.

But I keep walking, like Io.
       White hand of a moon
       slips into the night's coat pocket.

I have fallen, tangled in this sudden hem
       of darkness. Skinned knee and palm,
stubbed toe, cornstalks leaning like angels
fallen in the fish light.
       Their dry-leafed gossip. Tonight

       I feel their sorrow
welling up like blood and saltwater.

Winter Dreams

Let the deer leave new tracks in the snow.
    I whisper after them,
a whisper half-sinking, half-floating:
        Then carry your dark bed with you.

Your dark hair among the leaves.
        There, I touched your face
    and held your eyes shut. How they fluttered
and fought like thrushes
        beneath my thumbs.
                I wake in darkness again.

Listen, the moon is a knife, the empty lot a photograph falling into itself.
There go our faces,
        our children's faces.

I tell the hours like prayer beads,
    their smaller ringing

lost between shadows of oaks and the barn where bats are waking
    opening their beautiful,
            unlit eyes.

Let the wind sound and resound
    its soft obligato.

Small Breakthroughs

Two hackberry branches
            float downstream.
        Cutting ants carry late summer,

piece by piece,
into the earth. Hours slide deadbolts
            behind us. Everyone is edging

towards sleep. On the black rims of towns
        highways are crossed at night by deer, quiet
as ancestral ships. Eyes open
their small black harbors as the wind
            lifts the edges of our hair, moves the shadows.

You Don't Have to Go Far to Be Damaged

1
I found a trucker named Jim,
scaled knuckles, thin whistle when he spoke,

        drove me three days and nights
through prairie lightning storms
to that awful husband of mine
        living out his sentence

in St. Joseph. Jim said, take that child
back to Texas. But I had already crossed over
        those burned-out fields, made a promise
I meant to keep. His kindness made him old
and there was a stepping off in his eyes, in those
green suns, when we entered

the city limits. I gave him a white
moth's wing, and the plastic ring box
        I kept it in.

2
My sister slapped me when the rabbit shit
on her arm. Some injustices are too small
        to make their own places.
I hosed down the cage, watched
        the water enter clear
and exit black.

3

Blackbirds applaud over the prairie. I've had dreams lately
about hills that bask belly-up, a million years drawing
                        great breaths of sun. The landscape subsides
into flatness, unwavering. Jim wants to put me
in his novel. What color would you say your hair was?
                Blackbirds fall

in an ash-colored snow.

4

A February frost makes the grass
stand on edge. As I walk across the yard
                        for the morning news, my toes

cannot feel the rest of me. One end of me
now sleeping. The mind keeps working.
                How strange the body.

5

I thought about church
this morning, how to find healing from the mouth of the dog
                        that keeps snapping at me. My mother

wouldn't understand. I pull a knife from the drying rack,
cut the tip
                of my index finger. My son, now five,
lit with questions, wants to know
if I'm trying to kill myself. But I only want to kill this virgin carcass
                that reclines, plucked clean,
on my cutting board.

6
I want
to be blessed, burned
             into history and grafted onto the souls
of the suffering. My father and mother

would remember my name, would know
what all this nonsense
             means. I want my son to know
how far I carried him, through the summer,
the fields smoking,
             through the year's first snow,

in St. Joseph, aching, the moon
still broken and the two of us
             lying in a cold bed, one
not knowing the other dreams
about grass fires
             and her body dancing
touched in the flames.

Portrait in Black and White: My Heart Sits in Her Boat

Still inlet,
a mirroring, the gesture heartwood
or early winter rain.

My heart,
who is a woman, is reaching down to touch her face,
small hands curved into
       quartermoons.

Her body a black arc. She is not lonely
or brittle.

Because of this, just below the skin
of her reflection, fish,
       flame-bodied ghosts,
fan into waving skirts of darkness,
          waving skirts of darkness.

III

Sycamores

They rise out of coarser selves, angels of bone
in winter.

        They know all fragilities
of matter, how broken things pray softest, and when God opens
    such cold and perfect hands, it is they who answer light
                             with lightness.

Moon

1
There are mirrors
in my hands, valleys
gold as lilies
where our shadows go to break
their black bread.

2
As a child, I loved the smooth house
of my body,
slept in its warmest
corners,

away from the stiff body
of my mother's breathing, the terrible
clouded waters of my father's wishing.

3
The moon, my mother's secret wedding dress.

She swims under water,
I watch her white face scatter into tongues
of flame, angelic, forgiving.

Persepone's Blues in E-flat

Mother, you are a ruby in my darkness,
               steady rain of thorns,
        sweet black spring.

When you say "come,"
        the light in my face goes still, but slowly, like lilies
after a wind has passed.

Oh, mother, I swear
        I won't give in, not even to this snow drifting in
               from far away, veil to a blue sky
that presses softly against our hillside.

Even now, in my sphere
        of winter firelight, I am
your bundle of blood,
               your broken mirror.

Before the Last Day of Summer

The corn dies in its parched bed and sends a thousand dried-up souls
circling skyward. No one knows what will be left
                    unfinished—the sheets, great white hearts
pulsing on the line, a cup of coffee, forgotten
turned cold. But finally, this:
                    a manner of speaking, a tentative turn towards.

    And this shaft of moon breaking in,
walls white-washed,
empty, the window that looks past hills
                    shouldering stars to the south, towards home—
                                        more solid, more sorrowful
and my sister.

She must be lonely, eyeing the scratched pans
every night without love, each meal becoming an excursion
                    into dying. In my own bed I hold onto you, my hand
over your heart, quiet as wings ticking
    in the oak branches. I've done this for so long
and all I know of love is confusion, the twisted bedcovers
    escaping me, retreating as if every
touch is an animal turned loose with a will to run until it drops
or finds the field does not go on forever.

The Ascension

The spider rises like a crooked black star
towards the window. What a strange, short life
        trailing

a glassy pattern, despair and beauty
all at once. Soon it will hold
        the whole world in shining.

Beach Winter

Windows of gold light set against an unbroken
backdrop of sea: winter is only a small sadness, a list
of minor failures. The moon scatters a fistful of white birds.
All night they unfold, dive and break at the shoreline
or lie still in the tide pools. Sit long enough,
and something arrives, lovely in its unexpectedness,
like the slowness of a crane cutting the mist
or the shock of stepping into living darkness.
Then the ear becomes the ship, the wing stroke
of midnight crossings. Imagine horses blacker than water,
swimming out to sea. The birds, the horses,
the listener on the shore, all entering disorder, breaking
their ancient promise. The ship—no one ever sees—
pulls up anchor. Above the rigging, cold filaments of distance.

IV

Three Poems Beginning with Lines from Garcia Lorca

"No one understood the perfume
of your belly's dark magnolia."

Let me be the moon rising in the dark blue night of your throat;
let me be the daughter whose furious hair has suddenly flamed
    into flowers.

      Let me be a blue flame
      in a tree of blue flames

    "His heart was filling up
    with broken wings and paper flowers."

To my father:

One day you'll long to fall away into a casket of stars.
Even the grass will seem desperate, like the black flames of the dead
carrying you toward a gigantic past.

Your life will finally be
an accidental room.

    "Her voice left glass deep inside the wound,
    and a pale outline of bone upon the window."

I'm drawing a map because the moon
doesn't look for deep pools within the dreamer's walls.
    I'm drawing a map

for my mother, who wants to die
softly, to fall from her hips like ash and a small rustling of hair.

To You

Between us, between you
and the breaking shore my body is becoming, there's no forgiveness,
     but only
a woman. The brown moths of her heart
tearing their wings against teeth.

V

Narrowing Down

Beneath this river sky beneath the sky, there are stones,
grasses. You can touch them.
              Between the eye

and the stones
small fish burrow upstream in infinite
crescendo. You wait for first
              light to pass paperthin

where it never will, where shadows
remain shadows. You want this: memory pure as last
              rites—a first meeting

of skin with air, lips with breast, to go achingly back to a darkness
so complete it gathers and holds you in
              like an unexpected flake of clear light.

The Promise

1
The moon's pale hand around white trunks,
the shed's broken window.

Sometimes the memory of my grandmother
alone on the porch steps at night, staring into dark fields as she listens
to the sift and whisper of dry cornfields.

2
The hiss of a Buick engine
late at night, scattering all her little dustmounds
of silence. Some days, when her husband was gone,
she said the attic was full of birds
with stone hearts, that they beat their wings
until the whole house sounded like a huge heart opening.

3
Once I thought I saw them, dark shapes
among cottonwood branches, knife-eyed over the winter-yellow
     landscape.
Every evening I carry them home
for her. She counts the dead as they gather

and talk softly like leaves behind the shed,
loving only what hurts the young shoot,
the tenderest edge of her sleeping.

Four Winter Songs, First of December

1
Will there come to pass in the heart's month a day
when a savior comes wearing a coat of skin—
hand's skin, leg's skin, the soft skin of my childhood,
which has left knowing fields of wildflowers
and thick bees lay spread out just beyond her hard, living, hunger.

2
Who has been born into light without first loving the blood,
the darkness? Beyond the old blankets
and sleep-heavy embraces, wings of blackbirds stir
this dust layer of silence. Tonight, every star is cold,
sharp as the last prismatic breaths of the dying.

3
Every night, something gives in. Without words, I crawl
up a wooded slope, leaving a tenderness, my stubborn trail
to shine on the birches. My mother looked for me in the streets.
From there, she looked so beautiful with her thin robe
and empty breasts. I will always be her lost child.

4
Outside, heads of cattails nod like Buddhist monks in night's
dark temple. Trees turn inward, solitary and unenterable.
Buildings have fallen asleep in their soft coats of rain.
I have reached too late for the skin of your back. Now I have the salt
of love letters. Keep writing. In a stone's breath, we could be gone.

Nude Like a River

You only sought a nude who would be like a river.

—García Lorca

In my flesh heart, a lily has fashioned its glass heart.

This was my fault. I gave myself to a man who lived by the river. I was still so small: a thought, a fish swimming in his brackish blood.

One night, the man became a tree of blood-red flowers. He forced his stiff penis into my mouth. I still didn't know strange things were happening.

I wanted to choke on the black slivers of my bones. Every so often I give myself flowers, so I will remember my death and feel a boat of hearts drift out of me.

VI

On the Way to Enchanted Rock

I photographed goat bones
     under black-eyed Susans,
then held a torn paper sack
     while my son gathered white bits of vertebrae, leg
and skull.
He said they were lion's bones.

He found a round piece of bone I could see through
     and sorted fragments like a shaman,
the barbed wire fence
        behind him,

     baby goats and their mothers lying
on the other side. Near Fredericksburg,
        a flock of grackles rose, a black sail,
     in front of us. Surely there is grace near dim bones
blooming in gray tents of March rain.

Home

It's clarity,
    like the beech, still ghost
among the pines,

or a kiss, though not the first kiss, the over-glamourized
    kiss of one's self,

but the one thousand and first kiss that glides
so easily along the breastbone
                then downward, like a springflow
to the navel, determined
but not cold, the kiss of summer
    and darkening roses. It is the gathering

of buzzards on high tension towers,
                and the moment you think, why,
there are even angels
    for eating the dead! Or remember

your most lonely loneliness, the cruelest
jilting, or the worst lie
                and so the knowing better than to believe ever again
the lover's assurances of love. It is the way sometimes
    nothing happens, or that long lost moment
when we first crawled blindly
    out of the sea's black cuff—that old
sleight-of-hand—
    and the ache of never wanting to go back,
tender and unshining as we are.

To Robert, Waiting in Greece for His Bride

Things left ungathered, gather anyway. Your body,
     when I saw you on the other shore, had grown from its pallor
          to pure light,
all for the waiting for one to release her heart,
her secret.
Here I am, I promised,

not yet returned from nights under curved moons or full moons,
     hands drifting to another's hands chilled
by the touch of river
     and a strange faithlessness. I waited for suitcases, waved at you,
dressed in your terrible suit of moonlight. I remembered

another wedding, years ago, the young woman
who dropped her bouquet,
let fall around her feet everything she had known,

        her books, her friends, her mother asleep
in her bed of grief. The hour was pure, the groom
lost in the haze of the lover's gift,
            the lifeblood pouring out in a dim stream of fire
     only she could measure.
Even then, I knew I wanted
hands like yours—the turning of pages, the graceful finger-tracing
of backbone and thigh—to wed themselves to me.

        Every hour is a crossing over, from the old lives
rotting
in their basement rooms, the old lives chewing on nothing
     but empty spaces that once held them upright.
I walk dry pastures that stretch on until they fall into the earth. I walk
     barefoot,
        across slivers of bones that must have been me.

Suite: *Awakening from the Promise of Land*

i.
She lost.

Her black boat sits in a field of white poppies. She waits at the keel.

She watches from the sad rooms of her body, her eyes dark,
    two shining stones.

ii.
She sat in her room
of flowered wallpaper, cross-stitching a world of black orchids.
    I blame her

for being afraid. Now I give her what I can, these threads of light
    and skin,
        blood-hymns written in the room
where I cried like a child with that first sharp fuck.

She lost the world for both of us.
She lost the world for both of us.

iii.
The eyes of the birch close and leave her.
Birches sense the tenacity of clear weather,
        of sun-lit things.

She does not want to go on alone.

iv.
Step one: remove the right eye, look only
                with the left.

v.
       A swirl of gnats
       above a doe.
Step two: remember the face you loved first
  and remember how you felt when you hated it.

vi.
Her son brings a bowl of small hailstones
into the bedroom, places them
under her reading lamp.

She is writing a letter, a question:
What does salvation mean? The storm

has broken another branch
off the mimosa. Sycamore leaves
everywhere, and the phone call
from her mother. Did it hit hard?
Pretty hard, but the rose bushes made it.

These days, at least,
the everyday events are talk.

viii.
Night sifts its fine grain of stars
  on the water.
The heron on the far bank has long since closed in shadow.

She has tried to sleep with silence
falling from the eaves, but keeps returning to herself, shivering
from an inescapable rain.

In the dying hour,
even sycamores must wait.

ix.
She leans towards the window, pushing dirt
from the skin of potatoes.
She wants to say

  it is all right to leave, that she deserves better than this man that
      never sees her
shining slightly by the window.

            A fog curls off the black sleeve of the river.

x.
Because she becomes afraid of her skin, her body drifts
in a boat of wrecked stars.

Tonight, she will go out looking,
and take the cold as a good sign.

VII

At Nightfall

Weeping enters in, quiet as snow
settling on the still unfrozen
water. Stumps of trees rest apostolically, are softened
in coats of milky crystal. Will he tell us now
what he could not imagine then? That he wears on his body
the same scars that fly slowly
and steadily in our hearts, that each mark of grief
is a last meal under the late silence
of a low sky? He is nameless, he is a stone
apparition. He is his name, which means I am
and I am not the man like you. Perhaps, looking
in our windows he sees the stars sink back
into the skin of night and knows the fluidity
of his own image, what it is to be stripped,
his skin exquisite in the glass entrance
of wind, blood vessels retreating as we do
from the cold, eyes, hair, a heart
forcing like a fist every breath. We stay near,
held in the palms of our own hands, intricacy
flattened there, like dying on its black edge
of sleep. We stay because each year
something comes unnoticed, a winter arrival
etched in the stone-cold beauty of our bodies.

One of Three Possibilities

We must be animals, sleeping
as the air grows
cavernous, the ceiling slipping
into immensity. But we take

shelter from this
in our own small caves
of breathing. Snow flies

in the hill country, and night sounds
fade into a surprise

winter stillness. We must have
a kind of love, a word above
instinct, distant

and not yet solid. Look at this child's
body that grows between us, how it holds
yet cleaves the you and I,

makes the taut distance
slacken. He's breathing his hard demands

into us. In the air above his shape
we lock fingers till the hands
come to rest on the small
of his back. An offering, no less,
made before the onslaught of ice

and wind. Sheltered,
even he carries his dreams

to private depth. Set free,
I go too, feel the windows dissolve
into distance:

I am driving alone
towards a city, the night sky
lit with rain, the eyes
of the long wished-for.

Moving Out

Most things are best loved
at a distance. Even your own God, forgiving,
who presses his small diamond
of grace into your skin.

Remove him. Detach, and let him rise
above you, a cadence of flight
just below the yellow wheel
of lamplight.

And some hours are pure lapses

of faith. Remember the absence
of your sister: the Christmas feast
back home, your mother proud
before the table, tapered red
candles and gumbo; the ex-husband,

his brown-haired daughters
perched on his lap. Beautiful. Detach

and float above it all. You are able,
knowing you cannot draw
any of those hurt bodies
towards you. Hope for each

a love with ease, the kind
you didn't have. Your mother made you
so afraid of loss; no one knows

better than the women in their holiday sadness
what the empty air outside, the great
stillness settling among the pecan branches
means. A death is being sung now
within the circle of daughters.

                  Detach and sing with them.

Gathering Shells

There is the river and my son
standing there, the white field
of his back turned towards me, and midmorning
spun as a new coin on the water's shifting
surface. In the flash
he is gone, but appears
again, still solid and sure
as David, so beautifully sculpted.

This might have been a moment, given over

by another moment, or years before
while his muscles, still luminous
vines, shaped themselves to new bone.

It must have been half-spirit,

half animal, gone before him into the house
that would be his house, to sleep
in his crib, and to hear his name spoken
before my voice placed a Christian name

on his tongue, frightening him. All this

as if to feel the promise
of a future, standing in the river—strong
legs, broad face and delicate,
careful fingers that turn shells and their black
openings towards the light, to see
if they are empty.

Self Pity

So I am dying a little
each day. In this way I am not
so different. I read postcards
flying in from Utah

and California. The traveling
remember those whose lives are left

behind, departing
from their own hands, frightened.

Jesus

You are a surgeon of sorts. I open
painfully to each

instrument, though I can't see your hair

or the manner of your walk
among so many who love you.

Living Alone

She might imagine herself mist
rising like a golden eyelid
above the water. She's looked into
the river's own eye, hoping to find
herself, all blue and mantled—
whole somehow with many
great stories to tell. Then evening

will come and wash away with a black hand
any resemblance. But she is alone
in the good sense, with a longing
for stillness, and feels the hour when the railroad ties

hear their own distance trailing off like dark-skinned saints
beyond the hills. Outside, the air rattles

the mimosa, scattering its feathers
on the grass. There is a name for every
hour she's imagined herself a stone
or the water that springs
from the stone. Things left ungathered

will gather anyway, like the endless trails of animals
that cross one another in the dark.

Father and Child

If he could, in another house
of cleaner light, he'd be her hero and not the intruder
who touches her small leg just below

the lace pantyline. He wants to love her purely,
never laying his hand on her body—

just to watch her eyes move like sparrows
under the pink, marbled lids. Some hours
he can sit beside her, only close enough to catch
the hint of caramel she brings home
every evening. Asleep, she's the only living thing
reflected in his mirror, except for that pecan
where he first played his strange games, his daughter
still learning to walk, and where
he imagined his hands, filled with God's intrusive
flame, could heal.

God Will Harvest the Purest In Us

Goodbye to these houses
that heal no one. I refuse
the walls, the unhappy
rooms that spilled me into hot-iron
days, hours of blistering
prayers held to my grandmother's breast,
breathing her good life out of her while I watched
for the love of Jesus to relight
this place she was. I am so tired

of my body. I move without rising
towards the window, end where
my limbs, bloated with rain,
begin. I want so much to see what's left
dismantled, to know these palms
turned upwards are less solid
than the smallest believing. I want to lay such hands

on this skin, to let a river jump forward that won't find
a greater body than its own hysterical
beginning. To begin always, letting in
the blackest leaves and limbs,
already half-sunken houses, as if all
creation unites to leave its old skin lying
at the feet of its master. I am living

alone at the edge of her voice, binding
and unbinding her swollen legs. Jesus, what was

the voice that moved you so,
from child to man? It should have been water,
not air to which you were taken, somewhere
where we all might go, our lungs

emptied, our hearts lunging in waves
at the doors, your long silence
turned against you.

About the Author

Amy Randolph was born on January 10, 1966 at Sangley Point U.S. Naval Station on the island of Cavite, Republic of the Philippines. She spent her childhood moving with her Coast Guard family from state to state. She attended St. Francis Cabrini High School in New Orleans before moving to the Texas hill country, where she's lived for the past sixteen years. She received her B.A. in English and her M.F.A. in poetry at Southwest Texas State University and her Ph.D. at Binghamton University.

She has published poems in *Black Warrior Review*, *Peregrine*, and *Lullwater Review*, among others. Her manuscript has been a finalist in several national competitions, including the Ohio State University/*The Journal* Award. She recently completed her first novel, is working on another, and learning to play the violin.

She teaches part time at Southwest Texas State University and lives in San Marcos, Texas with her husband, son, and daughter.